Dedicated to my parents, David and Carol Ann Speicher, who encouraged my love for reading by their example.

ISBN 979-8-89112-881-1 (Paperback)
ISBN 979-8-89112-883-5 (Hardcover)
ISBN 979-8-89112-882-8 (Digital)

Covenant Books
11661 Hwy 707
Murrells Inlet, SC 29576
www.covenantbooks.com

Freedom Friends

Words by
SUSAN EDINGER

Art by
CLAUDIA GADOTTI

A plantation in Georgia, September 1859

"Take these beads, child, and remember me and the other women who came before you," whispered the mother to her daughter as the sliver of a moon rose in the dark sky.

"Mama, I don't want to leave you and Grandma here," the girl said as a tear slipped down her cheek.

Her mother said, "You must go with Pa, and I must stay and care for Grandma. You take these beads Grandma brought from Africa. They will remind you of us and of how strong and brave you are. We will miss you too, but your pa will keep you safe, and we will join you when the time is right."

"Come, Mariah, it's time to leave," her pa said quietly.

The family sadly said their goodbyes. They knew the journey would be long and hard, but they trusted they would be reunited in the future.

Westerville, Ohio, November, 1859

"Hurry, Anna Clarinda! Papa is ready to leave!"

"I'm coming, Mama!" Anna Clarinda bounded down the stairs.

It was time to leave for church. Mama had made her a beautiful new cloak for her birthday, and she couldn't wait to wear it. It was made of brown wool, the same color as chocolate, and felt as soft as her brother's new puppy. That is, when Clinton actually let her hold his puppy, which wasn't very often. Anna Clarinda's favorite color was red. At first, she was a little disappointed her new cloak wasn't red, but Mama said brown was more practical. The first time Anna Clarinda put on her cloak, it felt so wonderfully warm that she decided the chocolate color was just fine.

Clip, clop! Clip, clop! Anna Clarinda felt safe and warm sitting behind Mama and Papa in the buggy. The morning was cold, but she wrapped her cloak closer around her to feel its warmth. The click of horseshoes on the road almost covered up the occasional sound of Clinton's chattering teeth.

"Serves him right for not sharing his puppy with me." She giggled to herself.

Anna Clarinda was admiring the frost on the tree branches when their horse was startled and reared back, pawing its front hooves in the air.

They all held on tight while Papa held the reins firmly and commanded, "Whoa there!"

Clinton called out, "What scared her, Papa?"

Just then, two men who looked as if they had been traveling for days stepped out from behind the trees and helped Papa settle the horse.

"Sorry, mister, we didn't mean to scare your horse. We've been searching this forest for a runaway slave and his daughter. Have you seen them?"

Papa narrowed his eyes at the men and replied, "No, I haven't seen anyone on this road today."

One of the men stared at Papa for a long moment, then said, "We'll be staying in town for a day or two if you should hear news of them. You can find us there if you have anything to report."

Papa tipped his head toward them and started the buggy once again toward the church.

After church, the family was at home eating lunch when Clinton looked at his father hopefully. "Papa, I think maybe I should stay home from school tomorrow to start training my puppy."

Papa grinned and said, "The puppy will get along just fine without you while you are at school. You will have plenty of time for training her after school and chores." Then Papa's

voice became more serious as he said, "Son, I am thankful that you and your sister have the freedom to go to school and learn. There are children in this country who don't have that freedom because their skin is brown, and they are not allowed to go to school."

Anna Clarinda knew Papa was talking about children who were slaves. She had learned about slavery in school, but she didn't know anyone who had slaves. She had never even met a person with dark skin. Even though Clinton sometimes looked for an excuse to skip school, Anna Clarinda loved school! She felt sad to think that other children her age were not allowed to do something that she enjoyed so much.

Thunk!

Anna Clarinda was reading in the parlor when she heard the heavy lid of a trunk drop. When Mama walked downstairs carrying a quilt, Anna Clarinda watched her as she went outside on the porch and draped the quilt over the porch railing.

When Mama came inside, she saw Anna Clarinda and smiled. "That quilt needs a good airing out after being stored in the trunk!"

Mama put her hands on her hips and looked around. "Where are Clinton and that puppy? I thought you would be playing with them."

Anna Clarinda sighed. "Clinton wants to play with the puppy all by himself."

"Well then," said Mama, "I was thinking about baking some spice cookies. Would you like to help me?"

Mmm…just the thought of smelling warm spice cookies made Anna Clarinda smile. When Clinton smelled them, he would want to taste them too, and she might consider sharing them.

That night at bedtime, Anna Clarinda listened to the cold wind outside her bedroom window. She felt warm and safe, snuggled in her bed, waiting for Papa to come to say nighttime prayers with her. She heard Papa say good night to Clinton first. Although she had shared her cookies earlier, she was still mad at her brother. It just wasn't fair! He got to keep the puppy in his room all night!

That afternoon they were talking about what to name the puppy. After all, they couldn't call her *puppy* forever. Anna Clarinda thought they should call her Ginger because she was

the same color as the spice cookies. She thought Ginger was a pretty name, but Clinton said he was still thinking about it.

When Papa came into Anna Clarinda's room, he sat on the edge of her bed. He paused to listen to the cold wind outside.

"Papa, what's wrong?" she asked.

He took her hand and smiled a tired smile and said, "Do you remember the story we heard in church this morning?"

Anna Clarinda thought for a minute. "Jesus taught the people how to care for other people like feeding them and giving them clothes. He said we should treat others the way we want to be treated."

"Yes," said Papa. "Jesus said that when we do that for others, we are doing that for Him. We show our love for Jesus when we love others."

Anna Clarinda squeezed Papa's hand. "Papa, why do you look so sad?"

Papa looked out her window into the darkness. "There are some people in the world who treat others as if they aren't God's children. It's important that we show Jesus's love for others by loving them as He does."

Anna Clarinda's eyes grew heavy as she heard her Papa whisper a prayer that ended with "sweet dreams."

Scratch, scratch...

"What was that noise?" Anna Clarinda turned her head toward her bedroom door. The sound came from Clinton's bedroom. *The puppy!* Maybe she needed a drink or to go outside. Clinton must be sound asleep and didn't wake up to hear her. This was Anna Clarinda's chance to have the puppy all to herself! Quietly, she pushed her covers off and slid her feet into her slippers. She tiptoed across the hall to Clinton's door, hoping he wouldn't wake up. She slowly opened his door and the puppy scrambled out, falling into her outstretched arms as she crouched down to pick her up.

"Shhh!" whispered Anna Clarinda. "I'll take you downstairs, you silly puppy! Would you like a drink? Let's go outside first so you don't have an accident!"

Anna Clarinda crept quietly down the stairs, pausing whenever a stair step creaked. When she reached the bottom step, she looked over her shoulder to the top of the stairs to make sure no one had heard her.

"We will be back in bed in just a jiffy!" she promised the puppy. She set the squirming puppy on the ground just outside the front door. She giggled as the puppy sniffed the ground, running around in circles. *Brrr!* Anna Clarinda hugged her arms around herself as she glanced around in the moonlight. When she spied the quilt that Mama had placed on the porch railing earlier, she knew she was in luck!

15

She lifted it off the railing and wrapped it around herself. "Mama must have forgotten it was outside."

When the puppy came trotting back to her, Anna Clarinda picked her up and tucked her warmly inside the quilt with her. "Come on, you silly pup. Are you ready for a drink? I wouldn't mind a cookie for a nighttime snack either."

The only light in the kitchen was the moonlight from the window. Anna Clarinda poured some water from the pitcher into a bowl for the puppy. Then she looked around for the cookie tin where Mama had put the rest of the cookies after supper. She had almost given up her search when she remembered seeing Mama take the cookie tin downstairs to the summer kitchen before bedtime.

Anna Clarinda smiled when she saw the puppy had curled up on the kitchen floor and fallen asleep.

I'll just leave her there for a minute while I go downstairs, she thought.

Anna Clarinda quietly opened the door that led to the summer kitchen. She pulled the quilt tighter around herself and leaned slightly into the stairwell. Did she hear voices?

Barely breathing, she listened and she felt relieved when she heard Papa's and Mama's quiet voices. Surely it must be safe, but this seemed strange. She took one, two, three steps down and sat. Ducking down on the dark step, she looked under the railing and saw her parents and two others sitting around the table in the candlelight. The cookie tin and some plates were on the table. There was a man and also a girl who seemed to be around her own age. They had their backs to her so she could not see their faces. Anna Clarinda had never been so confused in her life. Why were her parents and these others sitting in their summer kitchen during the night when everyone should be sleeping?

17

The young girl yawned and leaned against the man.

"Oh my!" exclaimed Mama as she stood up. "It's time for you and your daughter to sleep now so you can travel when it gets dark again. Let me get the clothes you will need."

"I don't know how to thank you, ma'am," said the man. Anna Clarinda listened carefully to hear his quiet words. "I was so relieved to see your quilt outside, so I knew this was a safe place to get some clean clothes. Mariah and I sure do appreciate the food and having a place to sleep."

Papa stood up and stretched out his arm to the tired man, who helped his sleepy daughter stand also. When they turned around, Anna Clarinda saw their faces, and she was surprised to see they had dark skin! She had never seen anyone with skin that color before. She realized they were the runaway slaves the men were searching for earlier in the day.

19

She watched her papa help them crawl through a hole and into a secret room behind the fireplace. When the man and his daughter were safely inside, Papa began to fill the hole with bricks. When he finished filling the hole, it looked as if there was no opening in the fireplace, providing a safe place for the runaways to hide while they slept.

Anna Clarinda stood up slowly, stretching her weary muscles from sitting too long on the step. She turned around and looked directly into Clinton's eyes. Did Clinton hear what she just heard? Clinton put his finger up to his lips and motioned for her to follow. Anna Clarinda followed him through the kitchen, but before they took the puppy upstairs, she draped the quilt outside on the porch railing again, because now she knew Mama had left it there for a special purpose.

22

"Why are you such a sleepy head today?" teased Mama.

Anna Clarinda yawned as she dried the supper dishes and put them away. She hadn't yet told Mama that she had discovered her and Papa and their visitors last night in the summer kitchen.

Instead, she said, "That puppy wore me out today!"

Clinton had finally let her play with the puppy after school.

Clinton had warned her not to talk about what they had seen or heard last night in the summer kitchen. He said it was too dangerous, and they would get in trouble if anyone found out, so she'd better forget about it. Anna Clarinda didn't think she could ever forget it, not for as long as she lived. She knew how brave her mama and papa were to protect the runaway slaves, and she wanted to be brave like them too.

Anna Clarinda's last chore before going to bed was to gather the firewood to heat the woodstove in the morning. She slipped on her warm brown cloak and went outside to gather the wood. As she walked in the quiet darkness to the woodpile, she realized the lovely brown color was very dark, so dark she knew that she blended into the night. She was suddenly glad it was not bright red as she had wished. She knew it was perfect for keeping a girl warm and hidden at night, and she knew just who needed her special brown cloak.

Anna Clarinda was waiting on the steps to the summer kitchen a while later when she heard a scraping sound. She could barely breathe as she saw one brick at a time being removed from the fireplace until the opening was big enough for Mariah and her father to crawl through.

Behind her, the door from the kitchen opened, and she heard her mother gasp, "Anna Clarinda, what are you doing here?" She stood to see her mother and saw that her mother was carrying food for their visitors.

"Mama, I know about the runaways, and I want to help them like you and Papa are helping them. The girl needs a warm cloak while she travels, and I want her to have mine. Is that alright?"

Mama's eyes shone bright with unshed tears as she whispered, "If you needed help, I would hope that someone would be able to help you, so of course I don't mind. Come with me." Mama led the way down the steps as Anna Clarinda followed her. Mama introduced Mariah and her father to Anna Clarinda, and then she and Mariah's father started to pack the food for the night's journey.

Anna Clarinda and Mariah looked shyly at one another for a few moments. Anna Clarinda thought about how brave Mariah and her father were. She knew they faced many dangers and hardships on their journey to escape slavery. Finally, Anna Clarinda held out the brown wool cloak to Mariah. "My mama made this for me. I want you to have it to keep you warm and hidden as you travel with your papa during the nights."

"It's beautiful," Mariah whispered. "Are you sure you want me to have it?"

"I'm sure," Anna Clarinda whispered back.

Mariah thought for a moment, then she touched her necklace of beads. She gently took her necklace off and untied the string that held

it. She slipped a red bead off the end and handed it to Anna Clarinda. "My mama gave me these beads before Pa and I left on this journey. My grandma brought these beads from Africa. Mama says they are to remind me that I am strong and brave while I wait for her and my grandma to join us. You are also brave, and I want you to have this for helping me and Pa."

The new friends grinned at one another as they exchanged the precious gifts that were special to them, given to them by their mothers. The parents of both girls smiled. They knew they would probably never see each other again, but they would remember each other's kindness and friendship forever.

30

"It's time to leave, Mariah," said her father. "I'm ready, Pa," she answered, and she followed him out into the dark night as they traveled north to freedom.

The story of Anna Clarinda has been passed down in my family for generations. My mother heard it from her mother, who heard it from her father, whose mother was Anna Clarinda. One night, Anna Clarinda Sharp went downstairs to the summer kitchen for a drink. She saw runaway slaves sitting around the table. As the story goes, it was the first time she had ever seen people with brown skin.

Westerville, Ohio, had several stops on the Underground Railroad as runaway slaves traveled from the South through Columbus and north to Lake Erie. I set this story in 1859, with Anna Clarinda as an eight-year-old and her brother, Clinton, as a thirteen-year-old. There were other children in the family as well. The Stephen and Hester Ann Sharp home, built in 1857, was one of three stations on the Underground Railroad in Westerville. The house had an outside entrance to the summer kitchen, which was on the bottom level. The fireplace had a space where runaway slaves hid when bricks were removed. Stephen Sharp's will instructed that the *special* quilt should be given to Anna Clarinda. An old tattered quilt was discovered over 140 years later in an old trunk containing her belongings. I don't know if this quilt is the *special* quilt referred to in the will.

Common folklore suggests that quilts, displayed in plain sight, conveyed secret messages to runaway slaves as they traveled on the Underground Railroad. As a quilt maker and admirer, I would love for evidence to emerge proving that quilts did play a part in the Underground Railroad. Until then, I will enjoy the folklore stories.

Sugar and Spice Cookies

1 1/2 cups shortening
2 cups sugar
2 eggs
1/2 cup molasses
4 cups flour
4 teaspoons baking soda
2 teaspoons cinnamon
1 1/2 teaspoons ginger
1 teaspoon cloves
1/2 teaspoon salt

Cream the shortening and sugar. Add the eggs and molasses. Blend well. Stir the dry ingredients into the creamed mixture. Roll the dough into 1-inch balls and roll the balls in sugar.

Bake at 375 degrees for 10 minutes on a greased cookie sheet.

About the Illustrator

Claudia Gadotti is a freelance illustrator born and raised in Trento, Italy. She graduated with a BFA in illustration at the Academy of Art University in San Francisco, California, before moving to Auckland, New Zealand. Her illustrations are traditionally hand drawn and painted, Claudia has been illustrating children's books for over 20 years and she still enjoys it as much as when she started. Claudia also teaches art, part-time, to primary school children. She currently lives in Auckland with her husband and 2 dogs Bow and Bruno.

About the Author

Susan Edinger is a retired elementary schoolteacher who has loved reading thousands of books to her students, her three children, and now her five grandchildren! She lives in Millersburg, Ohio, with her husband, Joe, their two dogs, one cat, and a flock of chickens. In her spare time, she makes quilts and has a small soap-making business. Susan's mother passed along to her the joy that comes with keeping family history alive, as well as her love of quilt making. Both of her parents shared their love for good stories and reading.

www.ingramcontent.com/pod-product-compliance
Lightning Source LLC
LaVergne TN
LVHW061242040125
800464LV00012B/191